The Nature of Feeling

The Nature of Feeling

edited by Ed Bremson

Mijikai Press
Copyright © 2014 by Ed Bremson

Bilingual edition first published in Mongolia, 2014
Translated from Mongolian by Tuvshinzaya Nergui
This edition printed in the United States of America
ISBN-13: 978-0692238745

Mijikai Press
2901 Old Orchard Road
Raleigh, NC 27607
www.facebook.com/MijikaiPress

Editor's Introduction

Seven Mongolian poets – all of whom belong to the group "Beyond the Limits" – contributed to this book of haiku. As Editor, I helped with the English. As a haiku poet myself, I helped make sure the poems conveyed what the poets intended. To that end, I worked with Tuvshinzaya Nergui. She and I met on Facebook two years ago. Through that medium, we were able to maintain a back and forth conversation online. During those exchanges, I edited many of the two hundred plus poems contained in this book. We could have done the same thing twenty years ago, but it would have taken a long time. With Facebook we were able to have our conversation in something like real time, send files to each other by email, etc. So, the technology made this book possible, as did the efforts of Ms. Nergui and her Mongolian poet friends. It's not easy to work with a person on the other side of the world, especially one who speaks a language different from your own, but when you read these poems, I think you'll agree that she and I made a pretty good team.

It was a pleasure to work with Ms. Nergui, and it was a pleasure to work with the poems of these fine, outstanding, talented poets. Personally, I'm always attracted to new and foreign things. Perhaps that is why I became interested in haiku to begin with. So when the opportunity came to work with Mongolian haiku, I was eager to accept. One thing about being exposed to haiku from new lands is "what" they write about. So, with regard to poems from Mongolia, you can imagine there would be a number of poems dealing with snow, camels, horses, the Steppe, etc., since these items are common in the daily life of those who live in Mongolia. So when Tavanbayar Lkhagvaa says "a hungry hedgehog / scrabbles an anthill / silent Taiga," he lives in the Taiga, and it is a major concern for him. Another thing about haiku from foreign lands is "how" the poets express their experience. Mongolian poets, it seems, have a different perspective on things, given they live in a land so different from our own. Theirs is a society that is very close to nature, and so they relate to the natural world differently, I think, than we do. So when Sodkhuu Altanchuluun writes, "grief of a bird / who has wings but / no sky to fly," we can almost see the poet's mind at work, coming to terms with paradox and mysticism. The title of this book is The Nature of Feeling. In my opinion it could have just as easily been Feeling Nature. The Mongolian poet feels nature all around him all the time. And when he expresses those feelings, nature is usually part of the subtext. This is what I expect the reader will discover when he or she reads this book – a deep connection with nature, with spirituality, and with the feelings associated with them. I hope you enjoy this brief trip inside the arts and culture – and the minds of poets literally on the other side of the world.

-- Ed Bremson

Acknowledgement

During the last 3 years, after releasing the poetry book "White Silence" in 2011, our group "Beyond the Limits" set forth to study haiku poetry so that we could write haiku properly. Along the way many haiku poets, researchers, Zen teachers and haiku masters were following the same path, and we gained many friends in the bright world of haiku. We would like to express our gratitude to all these friends. We are grateful to Dr. Gabi Greve, who has been cooperating with our poetry group "Beyond the Limits" through the Facebook group "Mongolia Saijiki" since 2012. She teaches us haiku: its rules, nature, values and aesthetics. She is with each of our haiku every day and encourages us. She is our closest friend, advisor and teacher, and she did a wonderful thing in registering more than 60 keywords and kigo related with Mongolian culture, tradition and nature, in World Kigo Database. Now, in order to introduce Mongolian haiku to the World, we are publishing this book – "The Nature of Feeling" – in Mongolian and English. To fulfill this goal, Ed Bremson, a haiku poet of the USA, helped us greatly. During the last two years he was also with each of our haiku, advising and teaching us from his heart. So, it's a great pleasure to express our deep gratitude to our dear teacher Ed Bremson. Praying to sutra.

-- Members of the poetry group "Beyond the Limits"

EGO-CENTERED CHARACTER
OF HAIKU

As the philosophical concept, ego-centered character means "self-pondering". The most important thing for haiku is the self-pondering. The origin of Bashō, stated in the legend, says that on the basis of the feeling nature, he meditated deeply. And, what is the biggest "conflict" of the present postmodern period? Is it the effect of society and other things; or, the mind "Me" is exceedingly spread? From the beginning of the 20th century, the most probable answers have been sought. If there is the "golden average", "the attempt" to keep this balance sustainably is an effective method in the future. Otherwise, the future asks people to be "universal". Bertrand Russell defined "The gist of the matter, so far, is that a universal cannot exist by itself, but only in particular things" (Bertrand Russell, A History of Western Philosophy, 2013, p-258). As this definition, the most proper average and universality of human existence in its time will be apparent during the learning, recognizing and creating of "ART". Russell asked for the "term", so I name it as "the egocentric way of poetry".

Haiku poetry is an art. This is the way to self-pondering. This is the poetic form to keep the egocentric way. There are many explanations and theories for it. B. Yavuukhulan said in his essay about haiku poetry: "Japanese people consider the frog song as the most beautiful thing. So Japanese people await his song in the spring, like Mongolian people expect the nightingale song." (B. Yavuukhulan, 1990, p-134). Like this, haiku poetry has the sentimental and self-transforming character comparatively. The same is true for meter. In some ways, haiku poetry seems static and constricted, but this is a superficial aspect. It's the visible "shadow". So there is the term "Mongolian haiku" in our cultural study. Previously, the diversity of Mongolian haiku appeared in the haiku of poets from the group "Beyond the Limits". Now their anthology "The Nature of Feeling" is an anthology of "Mongolian type haiku". To be more clear, this is the desire of young poets who seek the "self-pondering way" to open the inside BEAUTY of NATURE, TIME and HUMAN LIFE through haiku. Also, this is meditation to keep the proper average.

Not only nature, but also the illness and wellness of human life exist in their haiku.

old and infirm—
my *teeth* bite *sand* in the dried
seaweed otoroi (Chinese cabbage)

Like this classic haiku from Matsuo Bashō, the sensation of time is felt in these haiku from members of the group "Beyond the Limits". The thought, "What exactly must we be beautified by?" cries from their haiku. Also, I felt the "intention" to involve life and its aesthetical categories, and their positive and negative judgments, from haiku of the group "Beyond the Limits".

Moreover, the untypical phenomenon of the language revives ancient information of feeling, and their poems convey the Zen Buddhist aesthetics.

cold egg-
feeling warmth in the forest
in the cuckoo's song

From this haiku, we can hear the legendary language of Mongolian thinking. So it's possible to consider it as characteristic of Mongolian haiku. Or, this might be the popular feature of poets of the group "Beyond the Limits". As the Zen Buddhist concept, when explanation and golden average is inclined, we recognize the "emptiness".

an old house
appears in the mist-
ours!

Instead of "ours" in this haiku, if it was "mountain demon", this is the deep explanation. Innocent explanation is the sharp expression of the desire of these poets to differ from others by untypical aesthetics. The spiritual aspiration to catch natural, inimitable moments is expressed analytically for these poets.

precious to dip
in a river the color
of sky

This haiku depicts not just the phenomenon, and analysis, but the advanced level of the poetry. A poet meditated not just on the beauty and appearance, but its substance. Really, it's precious to dip in this beautiful thing. The transparent feature of the spirit shines from this poem.

silent steppe...
blue feather-grass bows to
monastery ruins

The Mongolian feather-grass, like "dragonfly shadow" of Japanese Tiyo, depicts the sorrowful moment. There is no need for "additional" sorrow and meditation. The renovation is opened through the words "silent steppe, monastery ruins and blue feather-grass". Where depiction movement is, there the eternal moment is lost. There is the movement in the eternal moment, but it's not a mechanical path. It is the process to be expressed by strong spiritual imagination. The evidence of this moving moment exists originally in haiku is this poem. Moreover, there is the formalist nature in "The Nature of Feeling".

a poem
flies away from me-
fancy butterfly

A butterfly is the poetic idea by hermeneutical engine, and it has flown by the "hermeneutical explanation." So, just here, the schematic is implicit. This is the formal expression without the order.

At the end, what can be beyond the limits? The channel of beauty, that nobody opens. Beyond this channel, there is the universe nobody sees. The color and light of this universe is different and incredible from our own life. So, like the lyrics of the song of the band "Nisvanis"- "beyond the sun, beyond the sun, to the darkness and beyond the darkness, to the beam", "beyond the limits, to the limits, to the absolute limits". And open the newest nature of feeling! THE EGO-CENTERED CHARACTER IS IN THESE LIMITS!

--Batkhuyag Purevkhuu, Ph.D
Poet, Novelist, Critic

Tuvshinzaya Nergui

virgin spring…
the distant mountain vaporous
in the fragrant wind

cranes in formation…
is there a message from
my father, long gone?

april...
flurrying snow not reaching
the ground

spring
touches the tip of wind-
azure mirage

at dawn
the red horizon portends-
coming of a son

April snow
whirling in the air-
stirring sorrow

rooks cry
and awaken the sleepy sky-
light thaw

spring evening-
distant stars radiate
the light of memory

May snow
flurrying and flurrying,
it seems without end...

he went away
when buds were just coming to
the willow…

spring day...
shepherd boy touches
his last aaruul

early spring...
the universe crystallizes
in the first rain

still so blue-
pasqueflowers awaken
in the mountains

For Ed Bremson

Shelley Lake…
just understanding
why he is bright

For Nadalsuren

spring evening…
I'd like to pour wine for you
under this bright moon

For Gabi Greve

your traces
on the Gobi dune-
haiku lines

first fly,
beautiful with its wings
grinning

in the morning sun
monastery doves muttering-
limpid universe

spring breeze-
my daughter's hair catching gold
from the sun

my son
drew the trace of a butterfly
flower to flower...

broken egg...
the lama bird's cry
hangs in the air

long day...
the brightest sun discloses
my loneliness

a long year ago,
under these same stars
I bade you farewell…

afternoon...
an aspen on the steppe
hides its shadow

divine wind...
my ancestors' spirits
wandered

a magpie calls...
the blues in my heart rumbles
with new harmonies

full moon-
beautiful in the shadow
of the universe

melody of khuumei
flows through my heart
and recedes...

a black point
expands from the horizon-
camel caravan

limitless Gobi...
a herd of takhi reaches water
within a day

on Naadam morning
I wake up earlier...
silk smell

at dark dawn
the horse clatter receding-
wet eyelids

hot day…
shepherd boy staring
at a snowy peak

through the years-
there came eight horses
of happiness

summer . . .
a swallow paints in the sky
with a colorless brush

sunrise...
the paths of returned birds
becoming clear

this autumn-
flowers on my sister's dress
are fading too

late autumn-
Buddha merges with
fallen leaves

your words
rustling with the leaves-
autumn chill

I found peace
among the haunting leaves-
cold wind

first snow
on the fallen leaves-
dead silence

mid-autumn-
in the evening, the bird's song
is vague

from the mist
a roe deer calling...
how far!

your words
in the rhythm of the full moon-
harmonious

sunset...
over the mountain
red birds flying away

deep night…
a sleeping baby smiles
in the echo of snow

chikai bardo...
limitless universe before me
no wind, no sun

night snow!
throughout the universe,
only snow...

winter solstice, dzud year...
the sun rises brightly on
starving goats

White moon eve...
the brightest moon rises
in my soul

snow crumbles
under the horse's hooves-
sparkles on the hats

temple bell...
snow settles twice
on a bodhi tree

snowfall...
bad thoughts merge
into earth

Haibun

   I feel magnificent when I wear my deel. All arrogance and boastfulness burn inward and I exist gracefully and beautifully. Inconsistent thoughts and frivolity fade. My heart is filled by glory, respect, tranquility and all bright things of the Earth. I exist heavenly, when I wear my deel.

White moon...
my son courteous
with his new deel
   *   *   *

the last leaf
falling on the frozen earth-
new beginning

evening…
my entire soul whirling
in the snow

night snow...
the colors of the universe
only two

child's drawing...
expectation of summer
ceases

opening my eyes
in the unknown universe...
no left no right

Tavanbayar Lkhagvaa

under an old hat
very limpid eyes
gaze at me...

a hungry hedgehog
scrabbles an anthill-
silent taiga

taiga...
the setting sun lingers
in the needle scent

the east...
the legend closes in
and stirrups plink

the steppe is stirred
and past years revived...
tambourine throb

spring wind
lingers on the top of feather-grass-
long time

spring at the river-
a fish bounces
for the last time

the spring sun
shines on the scissors' blade-
a magpie lays eggs

spring wind
whispers new gossip
to my ears...

morning...
the magpie's call
predicts a guest

curious magpie
has asked the way to hibernation
since morning...

an ancient song
reverberates in the sky-
swallow in its rhythm

from the mountain
an unkind wind visits me-
wanders by my lapel

stormy weather-
spring longs for the snow
to melt

an old house
appears in the mist-
ours!

solitary wasteland
and dust of livestock feet...
stirred grief

so flaunting
it gleams and flirts-
starry sky

lightening
in the clamor of the sunset...
I close my eyes

a year went away...
someone comes to me
to walk together

all day
dragging my morning shadow-
longer in the evening

mountain and father
waiting for me to grow up-
become gray

through the open window
the morin kuur's melody is faint-
snow in the forecast

the limitless steppe
is stunned with heat-
wandering dream

cicadas shut up,
bobwhites crawl in the brush
their melodies resting

a black bird
flies and descends-
the sorrow

skybound...
how can my eyes become
as a soaring hawk's?

the moon stumbles
on top of the monastery-
serene shadows

long light-
a foal galloping across
the vast steppe

long song
receding to the distant steppe...
nostalgia

through the steppe-
a horseman receding
to the rising sun

corner of the yard-
boring tumbleweed knows not
where to go

edelweiss
eternal in time's flow-
silent under the snow

late summer-
a beauty folding
her skirt

flying over my son
to fulfill his desire...
a ladybug

doves
stooping on your balcony-
you are away

how cold!
bottomless lake
turning blue...

Sodkhuu Altanchuluun

this life-
a blind man touches
a cup of hot tea

waving ocean
in a drop of wine-
a tiny drop

sleeping
baby looks so very cute-
under the felt fox

snow!
a crow ruminates
in the white silence

time has come...
fear lightens
the darkness

cuckoo-
does not lay colorful eggs
in an unready nest

a descending crow
shudders by its shadow—
flies till exhausted

first spring day-
a golden coin is minted
on the mountain

Haibun

I just saw the end of the universe... My son
would like to live by himself for a long time. My
attacked words kneel before the heaven that divides
the wide steppe into two sides. Now, I am drying up
thus...

I am a drop...
the ocean is my
youngest son

*   *   *

silver steppe
under autumn's helmet-
plinking

spring snow
flurrying from an aspen-
no vigor to melt

desire-
well water not contained
in a bucket

naked moon…
heaving a sigh
in its light

thought break...
the scent of tender leaves
flies away

autumn
nestled in my
young heart…

insects
yearning for the light-
closer to the sun

I recognized death
and grew quiet-
my tea cooled

last rain...
each pitiful drop
shivering

a squirrel
meditating on the pine
without nuts

Haibun

Light sorrow... One morning, I see that leaves have fallen on the earth. I feel the grief ... but I cannot appreciate it and bid farewell to them. Autumn is a space that contains the regret and presentiment to awake; "How much harder is the sky than the earth?"

Most perfect figure and most fashionable colored leaves making a most perfect dance and turning and turning and falling to earth... I am sad... Do these leaves never listen to the applause? At that moment a crow is cawing.

Why is this call heard so melodiously? In the autumn, just like it, I'd like to dance, turn and turn, fall on the earth. I'd like to listen to the crow's call, "Hurray, Hurray, Hurray" and be peaceful.

cold wind . . .
a crow's caw appealing to
flushed leaves

     *   *   *

shell moon
moving in the sun's path...
what a beauty!

a ravening wolf
crying to the moon rabbit...
how empty!

embracing dew
flowers awaken-
dawn

stars
sinking one by one-
morning coming

Haibun

    This night, the moonlight is a little lower than tomorrow's, a little lighter than yesterday's. Tomorrow is a day that the moon will be full and my soul will be satisfied. Thus, the full moon looses, unreels, withers, flows and drowns in the deep darkness. Stars wait with bated breath and the moon rises and rises. Tomorrow is a day, the full moon flowing in the sky.

tomorrow
stars will gulp
the full moon

         *   *   *

spring
while everything awakens-
a beggar sleeps soundly

celibate sun
on blue moody sky
lonely...

trees
do not enjoy rain now-
it's late autumn

cold egg-
feeling warmth in the forest
in the cuckoo's song

on the last step
truth and falsehood blend-
karma blooms

grief of a bird
who has wings, but
no sky to fly...

blowing
dandelion moon, crumbling
as snow

deep night…
a dream of flowers appears
in moonlight

I am an orphan,
while I think of a moon
as orphan

birds
turn away for life-
fly away

Nadalsuren Purevdorj

evening breeze...
a thousand moons
on the lake

night again-
the shadow of the universe
covers my shadow

the playground
is conquered by rain and leaves-
silence all around

a dried leaf...
autumn between the pages
of my notebook

mist
embraces mountain-
autumn

leaves
withering on my palm
with memory...

cold wind...
in the clatter of the stove pipe
thought scatters

moonless night...
winter wind whistling
through me

silent steppe...
blue feather-grass bows to
monastery ruins

winter day...
how warm this stump
in the glade

spring sun
shines on broken dishes-
magpie's old nest

frightened sparrows
take flight suddenly-
quivering sky

under melting snow
ants awake in their nest-
murmur

first rain
blends with the last
snow

winter breath
rides the flowing ice
and recedes...

spring wind...
black beetle on
feather-grass see-saw

the sun blazes
on the mountain slope...
snakeskin

weary clouds
float through the sky-
moody weather

spring sky...
clouds splashing
in a well bucket

wind dance...
the top of the feather-grass
feels warm

green buds
paint my fingertips-
spring nuance

all day
two swallows carrying grass
tirelessly...

empty desert . . .
a lone aspen nears and recedes
from afar

early summer...
pasqueflowers wither
in the hot wind

sun bounces
off the boot bells
of my son...

steppe-
from the takhi's crest
a wild leek odor

child horse rider
awakens in the sound of grass-
Naadam race morning

downpour-
a little stream swallows
the new road

crane song...
a mountain slips into
the clouds

Gobi desert...
it does not touch my toes
the thunderstorm

fishing rod,
to disturb the silence-
is silent

in flying
birds flap their shadows-
noon

dawn glow...
the red road appears
before me

in the evening
ladybugs and stars-
too many

sandstorm-
the lizard-colored sky
whirls at me

thunder-flash...
river flow is divided
and soon quiet

moonlight...
a bat escaping
its shadow

stars...
twinkling to ask for a poem
until coral dawn

Haibun

The one perfect thing for a girl of the remote Gobi was the iris flower. I ran among irises on the steppe, swinging my skirt. I chose the biggest virgin bloom of iris and blew by lips to get the sound "zenzen".

Playing with happy clouds within blue iris flowers, my little fingers became white. My mother told me that if you cut the tender spring iris blossoms, the weather will turn dreary or rain will come. I believed her because it rained when we cut them. It's why I feel nature – mountain, clouds.

iris bloom...
clouds gather angrily
to the sound of "zenzen"

*   *   *

clouds
evolve in each moment-
me too

no traces
just red horizon and me,
sand movement...

swan
protecting eggs, her flapping-
turbulent waves

lake rushes
bow after the returning
birds…

Ido Nyamsuren

his shadow
stretches to the horizon-
dune sands

a wooden pole
standing still, does not wither
does not grow…

October...
the child with the water barrow
feels cold

September
with its lights and umbrellas-
how empty

a broiling day-
beautiful girls passing
like a cold stream

moonlight reflects
through the broken window-
a lonely robber

wooden bridge
slumps suddenly-
I gaze vainly

autumn morning…
my father gazes at me
in the mirror

a piece of candy,
to give just to my son-
my motherland

yellow garments
on anchoret trees unfold
to returned birds…

in the mist
my blue mountains
waiting for me…

autumn…
stars hanging
in trees

moonlight…
curious clouds bend down
to the well

winter night…
I'd like to tell stories
in the candle light

autumn evening-
everyone is drunk
except me

rainbow
on the distant mountain-
a door to heaven

baby's boot bell
lost in the camp last spring
rings in my dream…

a poem
flies away from me-
fancy butterfly

in the gray sky-
a feather dancing
with a leaf

a white hair
lightens my temple-
loneliness

fishbowl...
fishes talk to each other
about the sea

I bow
to floating leaves on water-
farewell melancholy

Darinyam Geser

spring wind...
the scent of new grass
is everywhere

on the balcony-
a pigeon pecks cereal
as rain falls

frosty morning...
a steed on the hitching post
dozes

black branches-
some berries
catch my eyes

bridle sough...
a smile appears on the face
of the sleeping boy

tears of
a camel who lost its colt
wetting the dry grass...

in the limitless Gobi
a mother camel bellows-
the road nears, recedes

a mother with a basket
glimpses a mirage-
great tranquility

snow shatters faraway-
a woman becomes mother
elsewhere

remote mountain...
a tearful old eagle
confesses

lonely grove...
I hear the clamor of
opening petals

full moon-
full glass of
wine

leaves
coming off from a tree-
freedom

in Khustai mountain
a foal of takhi whinnying-
shooting star

deepening
snow in the woodland-
praying hall

doves flying from
the top of the monastery-
brightening memory

October...
I forgot again to bid farewell
to summer birds

frosty morning…
a skylark on a branch with
the last leaf

wall clock-
the sound of a beating heart
in darkness

motherland-
squawking seagulls'
harmony.

clear morning…
I'd like to cry throughout
the universe

I bow
to what you are, poet-
eastern grass

at the end
of a long, windy day
chimney curtains waving…

spring day . . .
time stands still for the mother
awaiting her son

larks,
sun on the willow-
spring comes

melody of khuumei…
wings of birds cut
the sky

the thirsty horse
glancing at its face
in the brook…

crane song…
rain falling on
the pond

midwinter…
binocular glasses ice up,
migration!

sough…
walking barefoot
on moonlight

on this night
stars are countable-
limpid sky

beauty
dips her feet in the lake-
rolling moon

spring wind
touches the beauty's lapel-
how sorrowful

beautiful-
pasqueflowers decorating
the bald hill

bird song...
spring hesitates in the womb
of the world

stormy evening-
an old cedar frightened
by lightning

Burenbileg Batsuuri

early spring…
in the sound of splashing water
animals become strong

oh world! -
how beautiful the trees are
this morning

no rain!
under the holey roof
a swallow makes her nest…

as the river flows
a girl with an empty soul
is braiding her hair…

on a mountain ridge...
a family of wild horses
sparkling in sunlight

morning glow...
birds dissolving
in the lake

from under the snow-
pasqueflowers awaken
to greet the sun

precious to dip
in a river the color
of sky

sorrow grows
as trees become naked
before my eyes…

under the tree-
a leveret is hiding from
the coming rain

morning sun
looking into dew on grass-
sun-steppe!

autumn evening-
in a breeze grasses
dancing

ice drift-
from afar, birds arriving
in formation

darkness…
among the flowers, a squirrel
cracking nuts

knuckle bones
gratify and melt ice
in a friend's heart...

huug huug-
a little boy is cradled
during the travel

a deer calling...
snowflakes more and more
illuminated

autumn ...
blades of grass bow
in a horse's snort

rainbow…
do I see pearls there
on the hillside?

big big snowflakes…
how much loneliness
did they stir?

loneliness-
sounds of blue grasses
swaying

autumn lingers
with an abundance of flowers-
frostless morning

tethered to its stall-
a colt cries all morning,
all afternoon

morning sun shines
on snowy mountain peaks-
wild goats leap

beautiful-
the last snow falling
on spring flowers

Glossary

Aaruul – is Mongolian national dairy product

Basket – Basket is for collecting animals' dung.

Bodhi tree – The tree, Buddha meditated under.

Boot bell – Mongolians hang 2 little bells in boots of toddlers. It's to know where the baby is.

Chikai Bardo – the first moment of death, stated in "The Tibetan Book of the Death"

Deel – Mongolian National costume

Divine Wind – In 1274 and 1281, the army of Kublai Khan attacked Japan and was defeated by a typhoon, so the Japanese name it as "divine wind" – also known as *kamikaze*

Dzud – Mongolian term for an extremely snowy winter in which livestock are unable to find foodstuff through the snow cover, and large numbers of animals die due to starvation and the cold.

Eight horses of happiness –The symbol of happiness and each horse symbolizes certain meaning like freedom, friendship etc.

Felt fox – Mongolian people hang a felt fox above a little baby to sleep well. There is a legend that the fox cheats baby when he/she sleeps. If there is a fox, made by felt above the baby, the real fox cannot cheat baby and baby sleeps well.

Gobi – The name "Gobi" is a Mongol term for a desert steppe, which usually refers to a category of arid rangeland with insufficient vegetation to support marmots but with enough to support camels.

Huug huug – When camels are loaded with ger to be moved to another place, those who drive them say " huug huug" (хөөр хөөр) to encourage the camels. Also, saying huug huug helps establish a rhythm for the camels while they are traveling. Mongolia has nomadic herding, always moving from place to place to find good pasture for animals.

Karma – is the Buddhist concept which means action, work or deed; it also refers to the principle of causality where intent and actions of an individual influence the future of that individual. Good intent and good deed contribute to good karma and future happiness, while bad intent and bad deed contribute to bad karma and future suffering.

Khuumii – Mongolian national throat song

Knuckle bone – Mongolian children play with "shagai" - knuckle bones and there are many traditional games, playing with shagai.

Lama bird – Mandarin duck

Leveret – a young hare in its first year.

Morin khuur – Mongolian national musical instrument with horse head.

Naadam – Mongolian national festival, including three games for men-wrestling, archery and racing horse.

Shell moon – Half moon

Takhi – is a wild horse

Tambourine – Equipment of shamanist religion

White moon – New Year Party, as the lunar calendar

Contributors

Tuvshinzaya Nergui is a haiku and haits poet, short form poetry researcher and a translator from Mongolia. Member of World Haiku Association. She worked as an editor of the haiku and haits anthology "White silence" of the group "Beyond the Limits". She also translated the poems of this collection.

Tavanbayar Lkhagvaa is a movie producer and scenarist. He wrote scenarios of films "Big Dipper do not shoot", "Snow White", "Sinful turn" and "Heaven swear" etc. Moreover he worked as a producer and a casting producer of several films. He published his novel "Mist" in 2013. He was awarded by prize "Honored Worker of the Culture" by Government of Mongolia.

Sodkhuu Altanchuluun is a haiku and haits master of Mongolia. He is a co-author of haiku, haits and senryu anthology "White silence"

Nadalsuren Purevdorj is a poet and novelist. In 2012, she published a poetry book for children in Mongolia; co-author of haiku, haits and senryu anthology "White silence"   Member of World Haiku Association.

Ido Nyamsuren is an artist, designer, photographer.

Darinyam Geser is haiku poet and artist. He is co-author of haiku, haits and senryu anthology "White silence"

Burenbileg Batsuuri, a haiku poet and journalist, Member of World Haiku Association. He is co-author of haiku, haits and senryu anthology "White silence"

Ed Bremson, editor, is an award-winning haiku poet. He has been writing and publishing poetry for fifty years. He earned his MFA in Creative Writing in 2009. His poems have appeared in the Longlist Anthology of the 2011 Montreal Prize, Wisconsin Review, Bamboo Hut, Asahi Shimbun, Mainichi Daily, Found Poetry Review, etc. Many of Ed's poems have been translated and published in Mongolia, Croatia, and Slovenia. Now he has a full-length poetry collection, <u>With Dreams of Summer Stars</u>, that was published June 2014. Ed lives in Raleigh, North Carolina.

www.ingramcontent.com/pod-product-compliance
Lightning Source LLC
Chambersburg PA
CBHW051046030426
42339CB00006B/223